The Essential Sichuan Peppercorn

What Are They?
How Do I Cook With Them?

Xia Zhou Chiang

Table of Contents

1. Sichuan Peppercorns Revealed!

When it comes to unique Sichuan cuisine, this unique spice gives numerous dishes an exciting zing!

Before Capsicums (hot peppers, Habaneros, Thai chile peppers, etc.) were introduced into China, Chinese cuisine used the berries of the Prickly Ash to spice up dishes.

Originating in the Sichuan Province of Mainland China (hence the name), Sichuan (Szechuan) peppercorns are not true peppers, but the fruit of the Prickly Ash.

They don't actually add any heat to a dish. Most Sichuan dishes pair these peppercorns with Chinese hot Chile peppers, hence there can be a reputation of intense heat.

What Sichuan Pepper and Peppercorns DO is to impart a numbing effect to your taste buds that stimulates your body to think its eating something hot.

The flavor can be intense (green Sichuan peppercorns) or mild, but long-lasting (red Sichuan peppercorns). The powerful numbing sensation that Sichuan pepper creates makes it distinctive and unique. None of the other peppers delivers the same effect.

The oils and flavonoids that "Do the Dirty" are concentrated in the red skin of the berries. the seeds and stems are tasteless and are a lot like eating sand.

Enjoying Sichuan peppers is definitely an acquired taste. The intense numbing effect can be off-putting for some people. Like most exotics, it can become addictive once you become accustomed to its unique flavors.

The first time I made a recipe using Sichuan peppercorns, I really overdid them.

The effect was like getting hung over from a cheap wine: I was disoriented, light-headed, and in general, wasted.

Took about two hours for the effects to wear off!

What a rush!!

2. How to Use Sichuan Peppercorns

Sichuan peppercorns have a solid place in the typical Chinese kitchen and are used in numerous dishes. Essential to Sichuan cuisine, these peppercorns are also widely used in other Chinese regional dishes.

What are those black seeds inside the husks?

Those little black seeds are hard, flavorless and have a gritty texture when crushed. Good quality Sichuan pepper should only have a few black seeds left inside the husks. You need to manually remove the black seeds and stems before grinding.

How to grind Sichuan Peppercorns!

Grinding Sichuan peppercorns is a relatively simple process. First you dry-roast a small amount of peppercorns over a medium-low heat. Then you let them cool, and crush them in a spice grinder. Last, pass the powder through at fine sieve to screen out he hard black seeds, any stems, and other oddments. Keep the resulting powder in a sealed jar in the freezer.

Can you eat the cooked whole Sichuan Peppercorns?

Whole Sichuan peppercorns are used to enhance and expand the flavors of a recipe's main ingredients. We usually don't eat the peppercorns whole, as the resulting numbing sensation could easily overpower the other, more subtle flavors in the dish.

How much Sichuan Peppercorns should I use?

For most Sichuan dishes, only add very small amounts until you find what you like (or your guests can stand). Usually, ½ teaspoon of whole peppercorns or ¼ teaspoon of ground peppercorns would be enough for a 2-serving dish.

As the powder ages, it loses its freshness and potency. That's when you increase the amounts that you add to foods.

How to store Sichuan Peppercorns?

It's best to store Sichuan pepper in sealed airtight containers in the refrigerator or freezer.

How long do stored Sichuan Peppercorns last?

Ground, Sichuan pepper's aroma and numbing effect will decrease over time. Whole peppercorns should easily last a year in a sealed container in the freezer. Ground peppercorns will lose their potency more quickly. Use any ground peppercorns within 1-2 months. It's a good practice to only grind a small amount at one time, and use it all up quickly.

3. Selected Sichuan Recipes

3.1. Szechuan Dry-Fried Green Beans

Ingredients:
12 oz. long green beans, trimmed, cut into 2-inch lengths, blanched, dried with paper towels
1/8 teaspoon garlic salt
2 tablespoons Avocado oil
1 teaspoon Szechuan peppercorns, crushed
3-4 small whole dried Chinese Hottest red chiles
2 cloves garlic, minced
1-inch length ginger, peeled, minced
1 tablespoon low-sodium soy sauce
1 tablespoon Shaoxing rice wine
1/2 teaspoon sesame oil

Directions:
Bring a large, well-seasoned wok to temperature.
Add the beans and salt and dry stir-fry until beans start to blister and wrinkle.
Remove beans to a serving platter. Set aside.
Add the oil and bring to shimmering.
Add the peppercorns and chiles and stir-fry for 2 minutes.
Add the garlic and ginger and stir-fry 30 seconds.
Return the beans to the wok and add the soy sauce, Shaoxing wine and sesame oil.
Stir-fry for 1 minute, then remove all to a serving platter.
Serves 2

3.2. Szechuan Chicken Stir-Fry

Ingredients:
4 oz. green beans, trimmed, blanched
2 tablespoons Avocado oil, for frying
4 boneless, skinless chicken thighs, sliced into bite-sized pieces
¼ teaspoon garlic salt
¼ teaspoon Szechuan peppercorns, crushed
¼ teaspoon red pepper flakes
2 cloves garlic, minced
1-inch length ginger, peeled, minced
1 tablespoon low-sodium soy sauce
2 teaspoons honey
1 tablespoon Shaoxing rice wine
½ teaspoon sesame oil
cooked long grain Basmati rice, to serve

Directions:
Bring a large, well-seasoned wok to temperature, swirl in oil and bring to shimmering.
Add the chicken and salt and stir-fry until chicken is no longer pink.
Fold in the green beans, Szechuan peppercorns and red pepper flakes.
Stir-fry for 2 minutes, then add the garlic and ginger, and stir-fry 2 more minutes.
Add the rest of the ingredients and toss everything together.
Remove to a serving bowl.
Serve with rice.
Cook's Note: For a more robust flavor, replace the red pepper flakes with a like amount of crushed Chinese hottest red peppers.

3.3. Szechuan Chicken Stir-Fry with Asparagus and Cashews

Ingredients:

½ cup roasted, unsalted cashews

1½ pounds skinless, boneless chicken breasts, cut into bite-sized pieces

2 tablespoons Avocado oil

½ cup low-sodium chicken bone broth

1 lb. asparagus, bias sliced, 1-inch thick

1 tablespoon fresh lime juice

⅛ teaspoon cayenne pepper

¼ teaspoon Szechuan peppercorns, crushed

½ cup chopped basil

¼ cup chopped chives

Freshly ground white pepper

Directions:

In a well-seasoned wok brought to temperature, heat the oil to shimmering.

Add the chicken in an even layer.

Cook over high heat, turning once, until browned and just cooked throughout, about 4 minutes.

Using a spider bail, transfer the chicken to a serving bowl.

Pour the broth into the wok and bring to a simmer.

Use a chan to scrape up any browned bits.

Add the asparagus slices, cover and cook over moderate heat until crisp-tender, about 3 minutes.

Using a slotted spoon, transfer the asparagus to the bowl along with the chicken.

Add the lime juice, cayenne pepper and Szechuan peppercorns.

Simmer until the sauce is reduced to 1/3 cup, about 2 minutes.

Return the chicken pieces and sliced asparagus to the wok and toss to heat through.

Remove the wok from the heat and stir in the cashews, basil and chives.

Season the contents with pepper as you may desire and serve immediately.

3.4. Szechuan Chicken and Mushroom Soup

Ingredients:

1 – 4 oz. can sliced organic mushrooms, drained
6 cloves garlic, minced
1 tablespoon freshly grated ginger
8 oz. boneless chicken thigh meat, cut into bite-sized pieces.
3 cups low-sodium chicken broth, divided
¼ cup bamboo shoots, shredded
2 tablespoons shredded carrots
1 – 4 oz. can sliced water chestnuts
2 tablespoons Chinese rice wine vinegar
1 tablespoon low-sodium soy sauce
4 dried Tianjin (Tien Tsin) chiles, stemmed, slit lengthwise
¼ teaspoon Szechuan peppercorns, crushed (more, if you can stand them)
½ teaspoon Sriracha
1 tablespoon sesame oil
4 green onion stalks, thinly sliced
Fine Pink Himalayan Salt and freshly ground white pepper as you may desire
2 large eggs, scrambled
2 teaspoons Tapioca powder dissolved in 2 tablespoons chicken broth

Directions:

Heat oil to shimmering in a soup pot.
Sauté mushrooms until they sweat and lose water.
Add garlic and ginger and stir-cook 30 seconds.
Add chicken pieces and stir-cook until chicken is no longer pink.
Add broth, bamboo shoots, carrots and bring to a rolling boil.
Reduce heat to simmer, cover, and simmer 15 minutes.

Add water chestnuts, vinegar and soy sauce.
Fold in the dried chiles, peppercorns, Sriracha, and the oil.
Add green onions and salt and pepper as you may desire.
Bring to a rolling boil. Reduce heat to simmer.
While stirring the soup vigorously, drizzle in the eggs to form egg strings.
While stirring, add in the dissolved Tapioca to thicken.
Add more dissolved Tapioca until the soup reaches your desired thickness.
Serve hot.

3.5. Sichuan Chicken Spaghetti Casserole

Ingredients:
4 – chicken thighs, boneless, skinless, sliced into bite-sized pieces
1 teaspoon garlic salt
1 bay leaf
Water, to cover
8 oz. uncooked spaghetti
3 tablespoons ghee
1 large yellow onion, chopped
½ medium-size green pepper, stemmed, cord, seeded, coarsely chopped
2 celery ribs, chopped
2 garlic cloves, minced
1 – 10 ¾ oz can cream of mushroom soup
1 – 28 oz. can diced tomatoes, drained and chopped
1 teaspoon Worcestershire sauce
¼ teaspoon Sichuan peppercorns, lightly roasted, crushed
¼ teaspoon freshly ground black pepper
¼ teaspoon crushed red pepper flakes
Garlic salt as you may desire
Vegetable cooking spray
1 cup shredded medium Cheddar cheese

Directions:
Place first 3 ingredients and water to cover in an electric pressure cooker.
Close and lock lid. Set the vent to "sealing".
Select "Pressure Cook," High pressure, 10 minutes.
When the cooking cycle's completed, wait until the display shows "L050,"

Select "Cancel," and carefully open the vent to release residual steam and pressure.

When the pressure indicator pin drops down, carefully unlock and remove the lid.

Remove chicken to serving dish. Discard bay leaf.

Break spaghetti into thirds, and add to liner.

Add extra water to completely submerge the pasta.

Close and lock lid. Set the vent to "sealing".

Select "Pressure Cook," High pressure, <half the package cooking time minus 2 minutes>.

When the cooking cycle's completed, wait until the display shows "L050,"

Select "Cancel," and carefully open the vent to release residual steam and pressure.

When the pressure indicator pin drops down, carefully unlock and remove the lid.

Remove the cooked spaghetti to a 3 qt. mixing bowl and set aside.

Discard cooking liquid, reserving ¼ cup cooking liquid.

Heat ghee in a large skillet over medium-high heat.

Add onion and next 3 ingredients.

Sauté until onion is translucent, then add onion to spaghetti.

Blend soup and ¼ cup reserved pasta liquid into spaghetti mixture.

Stir in chicken, tomatoes, and next 5 ingredients.

Add garlic salt as you may desire.

Ladle spaghetti mixture into a lightly greased (with cooking spray) 9x13-inch baking dish.

Top with cheese and bake at 350°F. for 15 to 20 minutes, or until cheese becomes melty.

3.6. Sichuan Beef And Red Pepper Stir Fry

Ingredients:
1 teaspoon Szechuan peppercorns, freshly ground
1 tablespoon cornstarch
2 – 4 oz. ribeye steaks, trimmed, sliced into strips
2 tablespoon Avocado oil
1-inchlength ginger, minced
1 garlic clove, minced
1 red bell pepper, stemmed, cored, seeded, julienned
6 spring onions, thinly sliced
2 tablespoons low-sodium soy sauce
2 tablespoons low-sodium beef stock
Cooked ramen noodles, spice packet discarded, for serving

Directions:
Mix the Szechuan pepper with the cornstarch and coat the steak strips.
Bring a large, well-seasoned wok to temperature.
Swirl in the oil and bring to shimmering.
Add the ginger and garlic and stir-fry for 15 seconds, then Add the steak and stir-fry for 1 minute.
Add the bell pepper and spring onion and stir-fry until the pepper softens.
Add the soy sauce and stock and stir-fry to combine and to coat the meat.
Divide the ramen between 2 individual serving bowls.
Divide the steak mixture between the two bowls and ladle over the noodles.
Serves 2

3.7. Grilled Sichuan Steak

Ingredients:
1– 8 oz. London Broil steak
2 tablespoons extra light olive oil, for grilling
Marinade:
1 teaspoon minced fresh ginger
2 cloves garlic, minced
½ teaspoon crushed dried Tianjin (Tien Tsin) chiles
1 green onion, thinly sliced
1 tablespoon sesame oil
Shallot Sauce:
1 tablespoon peanut oil
1 shallot, minced
½ teaspoon minced fresh ginger
½ teaspoon minced garlic
½ teaspoon crushed dried Tianjin (Tien Tsin) chiles
1½ tablespoons low-sodium beef stock
1½ tablespoons low-sodium soy sauce
1½ tablespoons Mirin
1 tablespoon butter, melted
½ teaspoon fine table salt
½ teaspoon ground Sichuan peppercorns

Directions:
Combine the Marinade ingredients in a small mixing bowl.
Place a sheet of plastic film on a suitable work surface.
Center the steak on the film and rub the steak all over with the marinade.
Wrap up the steak in the film and refrigerate 6 hours or overnight.
Make the Sauce:
In a medium saucepan, heat the oil to shimmering over low heat.

Add the next 6 ingredients (shallot through mirin) and stir-cook until the shallot is translucent.

Fold in the butter and stir-cook until the butter is fully incorporated.

Remove to a gravy bowl and keep warm.

Prepare the Steak:

Heat a gas grill to 550°F.

Remove the steak from the refrigerator, unwrap, and let it come to room temperature.

Wipe off any excess Marinade with paper towels and discard.

Brush the steak all over with grilling oil.

Combine the salt and pepper and liberally rub all over the steak.

Use your fingers to press the mixture into the meat.

Grill steak to medium rare (internal temperature 120°F.), turning once.

Remove to a serving platter, let rest 15 minutes, then slice thinly across the grain.

Pour the Sauce over all and serve.

3.8. Chengdu-Style Gong Bao Ji Ding

You probably know this dish by its Western name, "Kung Pau Chicken"!

Ingredients:
Marinated Chicken:
12 oz. chicken meat cut into ½-inch cubes
2 teaspoons light soy sauce
1 teaspoon dark soy sauce
1 teaspoon Shaoxing wine
1½ tablespoons potato starch
½ teaspoon salt
1½ tablespoons cold water
Gong Bao Sauce:
2 tablespoons white cane sugar
2 tablespoons Chinese Black Vinegar
1 tablespoon Shaoxing wine
1 tablespoon low-sodium chicken broth
1 teaspoon sesame oil (alt: Avocado oil)
1 teaspoon light soy sauce
¾ teaspoon dark soy sauce
¾ teaspoon potato starch
Stir-Fry:
¼ cup Avocado oil
12 dried Szechuan (Sichuan) chiles
1 teaspoon Sichuan peppercorns
3 garlic cloves, sliced
2-inch piece fresh ginger, peeled and Julienned
5 scallions, white parts only, cut into ½-inch pieces
½ cup roasted or fried, unsalted peanuts
Directions:

Marinated Chicken Preparation:
Wash the chicken in salted water. Rinse and pat very dry on paper towels.
Add all ingredients (except water and chicken) to a 2 qt. mixing bowl.
Whisk until the starch is dissolved. Add just enough water to form a loose paste.
Add in chicken and gently toss to coat the chicken in a thin film. Let marinate for 30 minutes.

Sauce Preparation:
Whisk ingredients all together in a medium mixing bowl.
Continue whisking until the sugar and starch are dissolved. Set aside.

Stir-fry the Chicken:
Heat a well-seasoned wok over very high heat.
Swirl in the oil to coat the insides of the wok.
Stir-fry the chiles and peppercorns until they are just fragrant, but not burnt (about 5 seconds).
Using a slotted spoon, fold in the reserved chicken.
Stir-fry the chicken until no longer pink.
Add the garlic, ginger, and scallions, and stir-fry 30 seconds.
Drizzle the reserved sauce over the wok's contents.
Stir-fry until all the ingredients are evenly coated and the chicken is cooked through.
Drizzle in a little water(1 tablespoon at a time) to keep the sauce from clumping as it coats and thickens.
Mix in the peanuts and serve immediately.

"Americanized Version":

Ingredients Changes:

Marinated Chicken:
Replace potato starch with Tapioca powder.
Replace [both the light and dark] soy sauces with 1 tablespoon low-sodium soy sauce.
Replace Shaoxing wine with Sherry (or chicken broth)

Gong Bao Sauce:

Add 1 more tablespoon sugar

Replace Chinese Black vinegar with [1 tablespoon
Worcestershire sauce plus 1 tablespoon
Balsamic Vinegar]

Replace [both light and dark soy sauces] with 2 teaspoons
low-sodium soy sauce.

Add ¼ teaspoon garlic powder

Add 2 teaspoons ginger powder

Replace potato starch with Tapioca powder.

Stir-Fry:

Eliminate the garlic cloves and ginger pieces.

Directions Changes:

Sauce Preparation:

Whisk ingredients all together in a medium mixing bowl.
Continue whisking until the sugar and powders are dissolved.
Set aside.

Cooking hint: For a crispier chicken:

Before marinating the chicken, roll the dried chicken in
cornstarch.

Stir-fry coated chicken in hot oil in a very hot wok for a few
minutes to get a crispy exterior.

Add crispy chicken to marinade and toss to coat.
coated.

3.9. Szechuan Noodles

Ingredients:
⅓ cup Avocado oil
6 cloves garlic, smashed
1-inch fresh ginger, peeled, grated
1 teaspoon crushed red pepper flakes (more if you like it hot)
8 ounces Chinese wide egg noodles cooked al dente, drained
½ cup low-sodium soy sauce
¼ cup rice vinegar
2 tablespoons honey (or sugar substitute)
¼ teaspoon Sichuan peppercorns, crushed
1-2 tablespoons chili paste (Sambal Oelek) as you may desire
⅓ cup water
½ lb. ground lean (83%) turkey
Freshly ground white pepper
1 sweet Vidalia onion, thinly sliced
8 green onions, chopped, divided
4 baby Bok Choy, bias sliced

Directions:
Heat a large skillet over medium heat.
Add the Avocado oil, garlic, ginger, and chili flakes.
Cook, stirring occasionally until the garlic is fragrant, 5 minutes.
Cook 30 seconds to 1 minute more.
Remove from the heat and very carefully transfer the oil to a heat proof bowl or glass jar.
Combine the soy sauce, vinegar, honey, peppercorns, chili paste, and water in a small mixing bowl.
Place the skillet over medium high heat and add the turkey.
Dust with pepper and brown all over, breaking it up as it cooks, about 5 minutes.

Add the Vidalia and ½ the green onions, and cook another 2-3 minutes.
Slowly pour in the soy sauce mixture and add the Bok Choy.
Bring the mixture to a simmer and stir-cook until the sauce coats the turkey, about 3-5 minutes.
Stir in the noodles and 2 tablespoons chili oil.
Remove from the heat.
Serve topped with additional chili oil and green onions.
Serves 6

3.10. Szechuan Chow Fun

Ingredients:
8 oz. beef, thinly sliced
4 tablespoons Avocado oil, divided
1 lb. fresh wide rice noodles
1 small white onion, quartered
8 oz. bean sprouts, blanched, dried
6 green onions, bias sliced 2-inches long

Marinade sauce:
1 tablespoon Chinese Shaoxing wine
1 teaspoon low-sodium soy sauce
1 tablespoon oyster sauce
1 teaspoon sesame oil
1 tablespoon Tapioca powder

Stir fry sauce:
1 tablespoon Avocado oil
2 teaspoons light low-sodium soy sauce
1 teaspoon dark low-sodium soy sauce
½ teaspoon white cane sugar
¼ teaspoon Szechuan peppercorns, crushed

Directions:
Place beef and marinade ingredients in a sealable plastic bag. Squeeze the air out, seal, and knead to mix marinade and coat meat.
Refrigerate for 1 hour. Remove meat from marinade. Discard marinade, and let the meat come to room temperature.
In a small mixing bowl, combine all of the Stir-fry sauce ingredients and set aside.
Bring a well-seasoned wok to temperature and swirl in 2 tablespoons of oil.
When the oil is shimmering, add beef and stir-fry until no longer pink.

Remove beef to a serving platter. Wipe the wok with paper towels.

Return the wok to the heat and bring to temperature and swirl in the remaining oil.

When the oil is shimmering, add rice noodles and onion and stir-fry for 30 seconds.

Pour in the Stir-fry sauce and stir-fry all together for 30 seconds.

Gently fold in the bean sprouts and stir fry 30 seconds to coat the noodles with sauce.

Fold the meat back in, and stir-fry all to heat through.

Cast the green onions over all, and stir-fry another 30 seconds. Remove all to a serving platter.

Serve hot!

3.11. Singapore Mei Fun

Ingredients:
Stir fry sauce:
1 tablespoon Chinese Shaoxing wine
½ tablespoons light low-sodium soy sauce
1 teaspoon dark low-sodium soy sauce
2 teaspoon sesame oil
½ tablespoons oyster sauce, optional
1 teaspoon sugar
⅛ teaspoon Szechuan peppercorns, crushed
Making the Mei Fun:
¼ lb. dried rice noodles
2 tablespoons Avocado oil, divided
2 large eggs, scrambled
8 whole Shrimp, peeled and deveined
⅓ cup Chinese Char Siu, finely sliced
1 cup shredded Napa Cabbage
½ cup shredded carrot
½ cup shredded red onion
1 fresh green pepper, shredded (I use half green and half red)
1 green onion, bias sliced into 2-inch sections
½ tablespoon golden curry powder

Directions:
In a small bowl, whisk together the Stir-fry sauce ingredients and set aside.
Pre-soak the rice noodles for around 20 to 30 minutes until soft and then drain.
Bring a well-seasoned wok to temperature and swirl in 1 tablespoon oil.
When the oil is shimmering, add the egg and spread it across the bottom of the wok.
Let cook until it forms an omelet, using a chan to flip once.
Use the chan to chop the omelet into threads.

Remove threads to another small bowl and set aside.
Bring a well-seasoned wok to temperature and swirl in the remaining oil.
When the oil is shimmering, add shrimp and Char Siu.
Stir-fry for 30 seconds.
Fold in the carrot, green pepper, onion and cabbage and stir-fry another 30 seconds.
Cast the curry power over the mixture and mix well.
Add in the rice noodles in and the stir fry sauce.
Use chopsticks to toss the noodles to coat with sauce.
Add shredded egg threads and green onions.
Stir-fry another 30 second.
Remove all to a serving platter and serve hot.

3.12. Szechuan-style Chow Mein Noodles

Ingredients:
4 oz. dried thick whole wheat Chinese noodles, cooked al dente, drained

3 tablespoons low-sodium soy sauce

2 tablespoons oyster sauce

2 teaspoons sesame oil

2 tablespoons water

2 tablespoons Avocado oil

1 carrot, peeled, julienned

6 button white mushrooms, sliced

8 spring onions, thinly bias sliced (substitute 12 green onions and 1 teaspoon garlic powder)

1 red bell pepper, cored, seeded, diced

4 garlic cloves, minced

2 teaspoons peeled and grated root ginger

1 hot banana chile, finely chopped

¼ teaspoon Sichuan peppercorns, crushed

⅛ teaspoon freshly ground white pepper

12 whole unsalted cashew nuts, lightly roasted

Directions:
In a small bowl, mix together the soy sauce, oyster sauce, sesame oil, and water.

Set aside.

Bring a well-seasoned wok to temperature and add oil.

When the oil is shimmering, add the carrots and mushrooms and stir-fry for 2 minutes.

Add the spring onions and bell pepper and stir-fry for 4 minutes.

Add the garlic, ginger and chile and stir-fry for a minute.

Sprinkle the peppercorns and pepper and stir-fry to combine.

Stir in the noodles and then pour the sauce mixture and cashews and stir-fry 30 seconds. Cook When all are heated through, remove to a serving bowl.
Serve hot.

3.13. Szechuan Spicy Beef Soup

Ingredients:

1 package ramen noodles (any flavor), spice packet discarded
1 lb. boneless sirloin, cut into bite-sized pieces
2 tablespoons Avocado oil
⅓ cup yellow onions, thinly sliced
2 green onions, thinly sliced
1 stalk celery, diced
1 habanero pepper, stemmed, seeded, ribs removed, flesh finely chopped
3 garlic cloves, crushed, minced
¼ teaspoon Szechuan Spice Pepper Blend Seasoning (see recipe 3.16)
2 cups low-sodium chicken broth
2 cups low-sodium beef broth

Directions:

In a 5 qt. Dutch oven, heat the oil to shimmering.
Add the beef and stir-cook until beef is no longer pink.
Add the yellow onions and stir-cook until slightly caramelized.
Add the broths and bring to a rolling boil.
Fold in the vegetables and cook 2 minutes.
Add the ramen noodles and cook 3 minutes, stirring occasionally.
Divide among soup bowls and serve.

3.14. Szechuan Ramen Soup

Ingredients:
1 package ramen noodles (any flavor), spice packet discarded
1 stalk green onion, thinly sliced
1 stalk celery, diced
1 Habanero pepper, stemmed, seeded, ribs removed, flesh finely chopped
3 garlic cloves, crushed, minced
¼ teaspoon Szechuan Spice Pepper Blend Seasoning **(see recipe 3.16)**
2 cups low-sodium chicken broth
1 cup low-sodium beef broth

Directions:
Bring the broths to a boil in a saucepan.
Add the vegetables and spices and cook 2 minutes.
Add the ramen noodles and cook 3 minutes, stirring occasionally.
Divide among soup bowls and serve.

3.15. Chinese 5 Spice Powder Substitute

Ingredients:
3 tablespoons cinnamon powder
6 star anise pods or 2 teaspoons anise seeds
1½ teaspoon fennel seeds
1½ teaspoon Szechuan peppercorns (see Note below)
¾ teaspoon ground cloves

Directions
Combine all ingredients in a nut grinder.
Grind to a fine powder
Place in airtight container.

Note: although there is no real substitute for the deep, fiery taste of Szechuan peppercorns, a decent, milder substitute is [2 teaspoons whole white peppercorns plus ½ teaspoon crushed red pepper flakes].

3.16. Szechuan Spice Pepper Blend Seasoning

Ingredients:
1 teaspoon white peppercorns
1 teaspoon crushed red pepper flakes
½ teaspoon ginger powder
1 teaspoon garlic powder
1 teaspoon Szechuan peppercorns
½ teaspoon white cane sugar
1 teaspoon onion powder
¼ teaspoon Lawry's® garlic salt
1 teaspoon sweet Hungarian paprika

Directions:
In a small bowl, combine all the ingredients.
Grind to a fine powder with an electric coffee or spice grinder.
Store in a sealed, airtight jar.
Store in freezer for a longer shelf life.

4. Cooking Rice

There are three methods of cooking rice. The first is the oldest: boiling rice in a pot. The second is using an electric rice cooker. The third is using an electric pressure cooker. We shall explore all three methods.

Types of Rice:

Although there are many different types of rice, and you are free to use any one of them, I prefer only two types: Jasmine and Basmati.

Basmati rice is a long grain rice, suitable for every day meals. Jasmine rice has a subtle flavor that makes it good as an accompaniment for delicate dishes. Your choice.

Boiled Rice:

The simplest technique is to make rice in a pot on the stove.

Stovetop Basmati Rice.

Ingredients:
1 cup Basmati rice, rinsed
1¾ cup water
⅛ teaspoon salt

Directions:
Boil water and add salt.
For every cup of rice, use 1¾ cups of water.
Add rinsed rice to boiling water.
Stir once with a wooden spoon just enough to separate the rice.
Cover the pot and simmer on low heat for 18 minutes.

Remove from heat and let rest, covered, 5 minutes. Fluff rice with a fork just before serving.

Electric Pot Rice:

Follow the manufacturer's instructions and you'll make very good rice every time.

Instant Pot Rice:

Rice is one of the easiest dishes to make with your Instant Pot®, and also the easiest to make wrong.

You'll note that your Instant Pot® has a "Rice" setting. This is an automatic setting that determines cooking time depending on how much rice you've added to the Instant Pot®. You have no input as to how the Instant Pot® will behave when you select the "Rice" setting. However, the automatic setting is only for **white rice**. It cooks the white rice at a lower pressure setting and the cooking cycle can be much longer than you've anticipated.

The Instant Pot® is really not "Instant" under these circumstances.

Additionally, the "mouthfeel" of the cooked rice is unique to each user. For example, most of the recommended settings yield a cooked product that, in my opinion, are undercooked and a bit too "crunchy". I like a smooth, silky mouthfeel rice experience. In my case, I make my rice with a little more water than what other cooks recommended.

A search of the literature will yield myriad "recipes" for cooking rice in the Instant Pot®. All of them are wrong!

What tastes good to you will be entirely different than what someone else would prefer.

What's the "Bottom Line"? You must experiment for yourself, with your own Instant Pot®, and adapt the rice cookery to your particular desires and wants.

As I said, my preference is for a silky experience. Accordingly, I add a little more water than most will recommend.

However, there is an upside. A common ground. All of us agree that brown rice and wild rice, because of their unique structures, need to cook longer than the white rice. That's a plus: the cooking times I recommend are uniform across all forms of white rice and almost uniform across all forms of brown and wild rice.

The difference is in the amount of water used in the cooking process.

How do you proceed? You make trial runs of the various settings and see what you like.

I suggest that you start with the following procedure:

a. Start with a single cup of white rice (White, Calrose, Jasmine, Basmati).
b. Wash the rice thoroughly in a fine mesh strainer under cool running water.
c. Dump the wet rice into the Instant Pot®.
d. Add 1¼ cup cool water into the Instant Pot® and swirl to evenly distribute the rice grains.
e. Make sure that no rice grains are above the waterline, or stuck to the Instant Pot®'s sides.
f. Set the Instant Pot® to "Pressure Cook", High Pressure, 4 minutes, steam vent closed.
g. When the Instant Pot® beeps, wait until the display shows "L010".
h. Carefully open the vent to release any residual pressure and steam.

i. When the pressure indicator pin drops down, carefully remove the lid.
j. Using the provided spatula, transfer the cooked rice to a bowl and fluff with a fork.
k. Taste the cooked rice. If it's what you like, you're done!
l. If it's a bit too "wet" for your liking, reduce the water by ¼ cup and try again.
m. If it's a bit too "dry," increase the water in ¼ cup increments until you get a cooked rice that you enjoy.

The following table gives me the cooked rice that I like:

Type of Rice	Amount of Dry Rice	Amount of Water	Cooking Time
White	1 cup	1 ¼ cup	4 minutes
Jasmine	1 cup	1 ¼ cup	4 minutes
Basmati	1 cup	1 ¼ cup	4 minutes
Brown	1 cup	1 ¾ cup	22 minutes
Wild	1 cup	2 ½ cups	20 minutes

Pour the water into your Instant Pot®. Add the rice and swirl to combine.

Make sure that all of the rice is in the water and that no grains of rice are on the sides of the Instant Pot®.

Seal cover and set vent to "sealing"

Press "Pressure Cook", High pressure, 4 minutes.

When the display shows "L010," open the vent to release any residual pressure and steam.

When the pressure indicator pin drops down, carefully remove the lid.

Fluff rice and serve.

Additionally, I make sure to rinse all of the types of rice that I cook, even though some cooks will recommend not rinsing brown or wild rice.

Instant Pot® Jasmine Rice
Ingredients:
2 cups Jasmine rice
2 ½ cups water

Directions:
Place rice in a fine-mesh strainer and rinse under cold water.
Drain well.

5. Cooking with Wine

Drinking Wine for Cooking

There are Federal excise taxes on all drinkable alcohol products. These taxes are used to increase the price of alcoholic beverages in an effort to reduce their use. But there is a loophole: any alcohol that has been "denatured" is exempt. "Denaturing" wine is done by loading the wine with enough salt that the resulting beverage can not be drunk straight. All so-called "Cooking Wines" are denatured thusly.

However, please note that with few exceptions, these "Cooking Wines" are made from inferior wines. In my recipes, I make that distinction. Hence the admonition "Use Drinking, not Cooking, wine in this recipe," or words to that effect.

The reason is very simple: why waste your money on inferior products? By buying and using "the Good Stuff," you not only preserve the true taste experience, but you also reduce the amount of unwanted salt that "denatured wine" imposes. The cost of the Good Stuff is not that much more than its inferior, salted cousin, but the difference in taste is enormous.

Stick to using the Good Stuff. Your health and your guests will appreciate it.

6. Properly Seasoning and Cleaning a Wok

If you've never used a wok before, you're definitely in for a treat. Woks can be great fun and make exciting conversation pieces. Woks, like your Grandmother's cast iron Dutch oven, will last for years, take lots of abuse, and cook everything under the sun. Woks come in two basic types: non-stick and conventional. I prefer conventional: most recipes have you 'push the contents up onto the walls of the wok', something that's impossible to do with a non-stick - the contents continue to slide back down to the bottom. The conventional woks are either ribbed that tend to hold the contents, or 'hand hammered', where almost imperceptible 'dents' from the hammering process secure the contents to the sides. Both woks are good. I personally prefer 'hand hammered'. Get a wok with a "Steam Dome". You'll need it!

Whichever wok you select, if it's non-stick, it probably doesn't need seasoning. The conventional ones do. The seasoning not only prepares the metal's surface by sealing the metal's pores, it actually makes the wok non-stick! Like a well-seasoned cast iron pan, food won't stick to a well-seasoned wok.

When you buy a wok, it probably will come with a set of instructions that tell you how to care for your new purchase. It will also give you the procedure to season your wok. Be sure to follow the instructions.

Warning: Don't try to season a non-stick wok: you'll just ruin the pan.

Here are my recommended procedure to create a well-seasoned wok:

1. If the wok is received with wooden handles removed, do not attach until you've completed seasoning the wok. If the handles are attached, the procedure is a little more complicated. Wash the newly acquired wok inside and out with hot, soapy water. A good detergent is recommended, along with a stiff cleaning pad. Vigorously scour the inside to remove any residual oils that may be used to manufacture your wok. Dry the wok thoroughly with paper towels. Place in a preheated 250°F oven until too hot to touch. That will force all the water out of the metal's pores.

2. Wipe the inside of the wok with a paper towel or cloth dipped in clean vegetable oil, putting a thin coat on the metal. Place in a 400°F oven for 1 hour.

3. Repeat Step #2 at least twice more.

4. Place wok on stovetop and let cool completely. Then using only hot water, rinse out the wok, removing any residual oil. Wipe dry with paper towels and coat the interior with a thin film of oil. Wipe off any excess. Attach the handles.

Note: a well-seasoned wok looks black inside! The more you use it, the blacker it will become.

Congratulations! Your wok is now seasoned!

Cleaning A Wok

1. After cooking the food and while the wok is still hot, rinse the wok under hot running water. Use a bamboo cleaning whisk to remove stubborn bits. Never Use Soap or Detergent inside a wok!!

2. Wipe wok dry and coat the wok's interior with a thin film of oil. Place the wok in a 150°F. oven for 30 minutes or heat on stove until just hot to the touch. Wipe out any excess oil. Let cool and put the wok away. *You're done!*

****

Alternate seasoning method: Salt seasoning

An alternate method I have found to be effective in seasoning a wok is to heat with oil and salt. **Here is the procedure:**
1. Scour the inside of a new carbon steel wok with warm soapy water and a scouring pad to remove all traces of the oil used in the wok's manufacture. Rinse and dry well.
2. Place the cleaned wok on a stove burner and heat until just touch warm to remove any residual water.
3. Using a suitable vegetable cooking oil, like peanut, avocado, olive, or grapeseed oil, coat the interior of the wok. Work a coat of common table salt over the oiled surface, making sure that all the oil is covered with salt. I use a spoon to pour salt over the oily surface.
4. Place the wok on a stove burner and turn the burner on high. Leave on burner for 15 minutes. There will be a considerable amount of smoke as the volatiles in the oil burn off.
5. Remove wok from burner and let cool completely. The inside of the wok will be black.
6. Rinse out the salt with hot water and a smooth sponge.

7. Wipe dry and place on a burner. Heat until touch warm.
8. Wipe a thin coat of oil onto the inside of the wok. Wipe away excess with a paper towel.
9. *You're done!*
10. Now, every time you use the wok, wipe a thin coat of cooking oil over the inside surface before heating the wok. Then add what oil the recipe calls for when the wok's heated.
11. The more the wok is used, the more the inside will continue to blacken. That's the "non-stick" coating you want.
12. Never scour with soap and a pad.
13. Use only hot water and a bamboo whisk to clean the wok.
14. Always wipe your wok dry and add a coating of oil after rinsing.

7. Recommended Substitutions

Recipe Ingredient	Substitute
Chinese Black Mushrooms	Portobello Mushrooms
Napa Cabbage	Bok Choy
Bok Choy	Romaine Lettuce
Chinese Shaoxing/Rice Wine	Dry Sherry/Mirin
Dark/light soy sauces	Dark/Light low-sodium soy sauces
ginkgo nuts	cashew nuts
Spring Onions	(2 green onions + 1 mashed garlic clove) for each spring onion
Chinese style flat noodles	fettuccini
Squid (calamari)	oysters
sea scallops	bay scallops
Szechuan peppercorns	Szechuan peppercorns (no substitution -buy on-line)
dried shiitake mushrooms	dried portobello mushrooms
Chinese long green beans	uncut green beans
Chinese Sausage (lop cheong)	Pork sausage
mung bean sprouts	bean sprouts
Mirin	Karo clear corn syrup
Habanero Pepper	Jalapeno Pepper

8. A Final Note

Thank you, again for considering my *The Essential Sichuan Peppercorn*. I hope that your journey through these recipes culled from ancient China has been profitable. These recipes have been carefully assembled with your success in mind. Feel free to experiment. Add your own favorite ingredients, cut others. Slice the meats thin or thick. Remember, The Great Wall wasn't built in a weekend!!

I need to ask you a favor. If you're so inclined, I'd love a rating and a review of *The Essential Sichuan Peppercorn*. Love it, hated it–I'd just enjoy your feedback.

As you may have gleaned from my books, reviews can be tough to come by these days. You, the reader, have the power to make or break a book. If you have the time, please leave a review on Amazon.

Thank you so much for reading *The Essential Sichuan Peppercorn* and for spending time with me.

In gratitude,

Made in United States
North Haven, CT
23 January 2023

31487745R00029